Brooklyn Astronaut

Inspirational Poems For Kids

WRITTEN BY JERMAIN O. SMITH

ILLUSTRATED BY TANEICHA S. THOMAS

YOU'RE OUT OF THIS WORLD!

Dedication

I Dedicate this children's book to young teens and adults alike who are pursuing their dreams. Your life experiences will help develop strong work ethic to be an artist or an astronaut. Be honest with Yourself, be vilagaiant, and don't forget to take God with you.

I also want To dedicate this children's book to my personal Lord and Savior Jesus Christ. For without him this project would not have been possible.
I wrote and completed this book of Brooklyn Astronaut INSPIRATIONAL POEMS FOR KIDS and adults alike during a very difficult time in my life. And the Lord has not only substained me, but let me see my gifts become a light through my words and rhythm to inspire you to plan for your greatness, work hard, pray hard, persevere harder, stay consistent, dedicated, and invest in yourself.

Failure is nothing more then the field of gold mines, full of lessons we stopped digging for. - Jermain O. Smith

No Limit's	43
New Beginnings	47
Don't Forgt To Plan	51
Dont Forget To Pray	54
Dont Forget To Study Hard	58
The Beauty Of Your Imagination	63
Soar High	68
Student	75
Journaling	80
How are we doing	83

Table of Contents

Dedication 1

Message from the Heart 2

When the Earth Was Alone 4

Dream Big 8

Live the Dream 12

You Can Do It 16

Never Give Up 22

The Magic of Believing 32

Keep Climbing 37

Almost There 40

Brooklyn Astronaut Inspirational Poems For Kids
Copyright 2024 Library of
Congress.

All rights reserved to CEO Jermain Smith of Smith Prudent Reads Publishing Company.

No artwork, writing, or anything produced in this project, Brooklyn Astronaut Inspirational Poems For Kids, may be copied, recorded, or massively produced without the owner's consent, in physical writing by a letter. Registered with the Library of Congress.

ISBN's: 979-8-9853866-1-5 (hardcover) | 979-8-9853866-2-2 (paperback) | 979-8-9853866-3-9 (ebook) | 979-8-9853866-4-6 (audio)

Publisher's Cataloging-in-Publication Data

Names: Smith, Jermain O., author

Title: Brooklyn Astronaut : Inspirational Poems for Kids / Jermain O. Smith.
Series: Brooklyn Astronaut Dream Big
Description: Brooklyn, NY: Smith Prudent Reads Publishing, 2024. | Summary: Inspirational poetry about astronauts, the moon, and imagination.

Identifiers: ISBN: 979-8-9853866-1-5 (hardcover) | 979-8-9853866-2-2 (paperback) | 979-8-9853866-3-9 (ebook) | 979-8-9853866-4-6 (audio)

Subjects: Children dreaming| Moon--Juvenile poetry. | Astronauts--Juvenile poetry. | New York (State)--New York—Brooklyn--Juvenile poetry. | Bedford-Stuyvesant (New York, N.Y.)--Juvenile poetry. | Children's poetry. | JUVENILE FICTION / Poetry

Classification: LCC PZ7.S65143 Br 2024 | DDC 811.6--dc23

Edited By: Taneicha S. Thomas

Publish by Smith Prudent Reads Publishing LLC,

Brooklyn, New York

A Message From The Heart

In this inspirational series of poetry for kids & young adults alike, we want to encourage you through reading. We hope it lifts your spirits and clears your mind of wasted space.

Promoting positive lifestyle and sparking curiosity. Creative gems in your heart and mind. Put your space boots on, and only stop for new levels of success and watch the STARS!!

Stay focused to be grounded, organized, and sturdy with diet and exercise. Train like the champions and FLY like the Eagles!

Brooklyn Astronaut

Inspirational Poems For Kids

When The Earth Was Alone

When the Earth was alone
It stood in darkness without
the Moon.

When the Earth was alone
the lands felt the dry heat
from the scorching Sun.

Raging from the Universe
imbalanced, this is the
collateral damage.

Inspirational Poems for Girls

Bruised and burnt lands, abandoned Stars to stand in support of this Earth left all alone.

Run down habitats, flooding mushy grass, disguised mask amongst trees without leaves.

Hunted down species, wasted food sources, honey spilled over from natural beehives.

When the Earth was Alone, cut off from the Universe, it was

Where The Earth was Alone

reborn as a new Earth in a new Universe.

With a new Sun & Moon to nurture its core and trillions of Stars shining in support of its new growth.

When the Earth was Alone it healed scorched lands.

It rebuilt damaged property, flooding lands with flourishing wildflowers swaying in its splendor of fields with the bending of the Wind.

Inspirational Poems For Boys

When the Earth was Alone,
it formed new
mountains, highlands, new foods
to support new planets to thrive!

When the Earth Was Alone,
it built an unbreakable back
bone.

The goodness of Earth's core
rebirth itsself deep in the soil
that was sown.

When the Earth Was Alone.

Dream Big

Expand and pivot the mind.
Take it all in,
rest in &

Do it again!
This is the magic!

Venture out to explore nicer areas, restaurants, mother nature's beautiful open spaces.

The journey you embark on, is enjoyed when you widen the scope of the Space around you.

Inspirational Poems For Boys

Stay free-floating with your thinking never let your mind burn out and never shine again keep the boat afloat.

Aspire to be the greatest of all times! If you don't quit on yourself, you'll become a G.O.A.T for your passion! Go find it! Don't sweat it, you will slip & fall, it's the pits at the bottom.

But in the meantime.....Meditate for a little while, just sit alone, think of no trouble,

Dream Big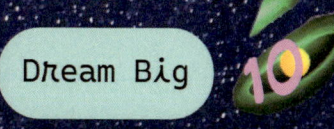

you'll find the answer that gets you out of that crater of problems soon! The how will be discovered!

New happier thoughts collected and more fresh air will help you claim every idea you want to achieve.
The World is Yours!

So Dream Big, expand like the crafted wings of a plane. But, check the wing span often and soar to the Big blue beautiful Sky! Thinking Big strengthens your

Inspirational Poems For Boys

faith, mind & soul become fearless. No push backs or tight ropes, let your inner child roam far like parrots at sea carefree.

On another journey of Big Dreams that never ends!

Full of life another purpose has begun, like a season of flowers in spring that blossom.

Or in a hot air balloon with a silly clown. Keep creating and adding to your Big Dreams.

Live The Dream

Don't just Dream Big,
Live the Dreams!

Spoil yourself like your favorite scoop of ice cream.

Staying consistent aligning inner strength you can rely on and trust.

Having goals with a definite Why. Everyone you love may not come by. You're going to spread your wings and fly!

Inspirational Poems For Boys

Get prepared to say a hard good bye, it's part of the challenging journey.

And Soar to the heights as far as the Moon & Stars. The dream is Real, it needs your creativity to hold temporarily.

Be patient let it grow and stand ready to go!!

Eliminate any fears you're a Giant! The Big Polar Bear to be revered.

Living The Dream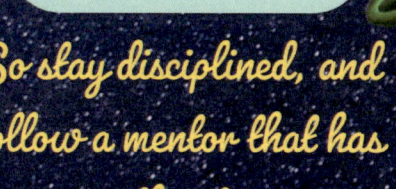

So stay disciplined, and follow a mentor that has proven authority.

Your mentor is suppose to find your faults don't let it be disheartening.

Pay attention and listen, while your peers parlay in distraction.

While others become lily lacker's,

Inspirational Poems For Boys

you'll stand tall like a tree in all seasons because you took daily action!

Pretty soon, you'll go from weary thoughts to skipping steps & smiling.

Living the dream in your purpose, dancing, rejoicing and living the rest of your life as a Champion.

Living the Dream.

You Can Do It

God has given you everything you need to succeed.

Our brain, hands, eyes, and feet are precious tangible gifts!

All other gifts and talents are great bonuses to inherit.

A can do attitude requires belief in your Abilities to work hard and your passion.

Inspirational Poems For Boys

Don't be swayed from greatness, instead be prudent and read often.

Real champions, sometimes bleed going without wants and needs.

Sacrifices to be a warrior requires, praying knees & hands working together.

You were given different tools than our forefathers.

You Can Do It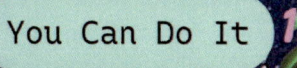

Persevere, work hard and keep a beautiful heart, mind and spirit.

Use the steam that made you mad in a positive light. Using it as a tool to stay strong and stay in your purpose.

Check on your progress, in moments you grow impatient, lonely or sad, your destiny is quickly calling.

Inspirational Poems For Boys

Make haste to catch your spaceship. You can do it you got this. Keep working late in your lab.

.Let the naysayers stare. Let your silent work ethic speak for itself, like a sword quiet & strong.

Let it be the only thing that brags on your accomplishments and why you are great.

Young Kings protect your Kingdom with Class don't be a brute in your community.

You Can Do It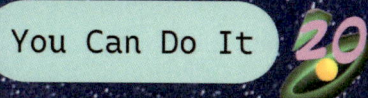

You can do it, you hold
brilliant ideas & dreams,
like sweet marshmallows
& hot cocoa in a Brooklyn
Astronaut mug.

You can do it. Don't shrug
your destiny off like an annoying
bug or gnat.

Start working, researching
for your personal styles,
Like NAS the rapper,

Be Illmatic!

Inspirational Poems For Boys

Your breakthrough, will be as beautiful as a spring sunrise paints the sky with pink, orange and white before it turns morning blue.

You got what it takes, you can & will do it!

All that's left now is to apply and simply do.

Never Give Up

Staying in it for the long haul. This is not a race, But a marathon.

So don't forget to budget your time, breathe slowly and take in deep breaths.

Inspirational Poems For Boys

Sweat rolling down your back, legs and hands, as you ponder a path and choose the lane to get you there.

Hate from others can't prosper because God Is with you all the time.

Use your divine gifts placed in your hands, words and lifetime itself.

Stay in prayer when you need real support.

Never Give Up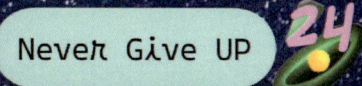

The One who created mountains and heavens over the seas, surely is able to take care of all his creations.

Hardships is life doing you a favor, so your future you can distinguish who's real.

Keep real cheerleaders & leaders around. Trust God first then yourself, he won't let you down.

Inspirational Poems For Boys

People you admire who are thriving will aide in your journey!
Mentors you can actually reach out to and get on the phone.

Don't seek them out, be patient let they will present themselves like the Elf on the Shelf.

Never Give Up, Let the chaos fuel your determination to win.

Never Give UP 26

Through harsh hurricane winds, stand firm and prove them wrong. Never Give Up!

We all have growing pains and trails at some point.

Just hold on to the rope of faith, and pull yourself up for small dreams & Big Dreams.

Here I am, currently, sick often & disabled from an injury to my head.

Inspirational Poems For Boys

I felt betrayed and alone, labeled an outlaw, outcast, just another punching bag at home.

Some will speak down to you, but their self-esteem is low, and they could never go where you are going.

It makes them feel good if they distract you from your dreams and goals!

Be firm Be Bold!

Never Give UP

God is first on your team, alway Keep him first in all you do.

Because you have purpose and authority over your life, you are no ones punching bag or door mat to spite.

Your life is more than love bombs, triggers or land mines of emotional stigmas.
You are as important as the air you breathe!

Inspirational Poems For Boys

Don't let the Darkness enrage you.
Don't change, and know that you are
King ready to reign over your Kingdom!
Always qualify who can be close to you.
You have the light within they are attracted to!
This is a battle, they can't win.
God made you a champion.
Your a light house that shines in good and bad weather,
Keep Shining.
Let no one tame, blame or game you out of your passion.

Never Give UP

Continue to be real and authentic for you, always bet on You!

Never Give Up, once you learn how to build a kingdom they can never take those skills away from you.

Taking time to find your greatness is why Shields & Richardson are World Class Acts. Remember they were once unknown with a passion. Find what drives you.

Never Give Up!

Inspirational Poems For Boys

SHARE YOUR JOURNEY NOT JOURNAL

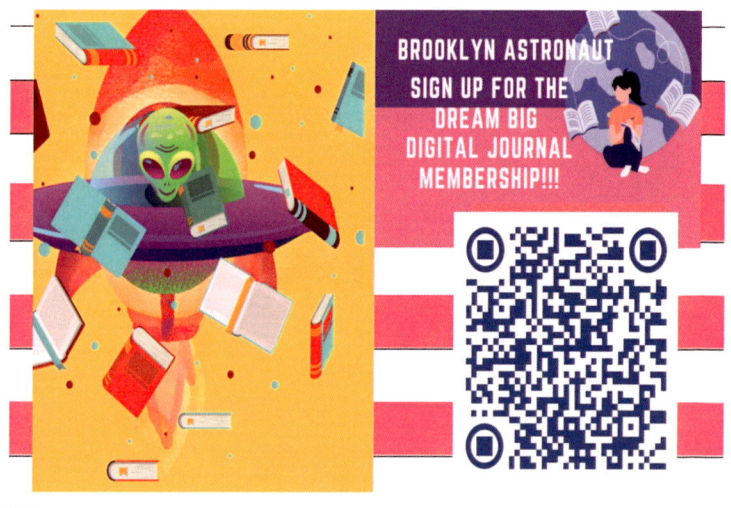

Journal your Dreams- Goals, Aspirations

Journal your Dreams- Goals, Aspirations
Journal your Dreams- Goals, Aspirations
Journal your Dreams- Goals, Aspirations
Journal your Dreams- Goals, Aspirations
Journal your Dreams- Goals, Aspirations
Journal your Dreams- Goals, Aspirations

The Magic Of Believing

The Magic of Believing
has my soul in a joyous
gleam.

I feel like I'm bouncing
from star to star.

As I skip & sing,and
shine like Bling Bling.

From a Prince or
Princess
and a King or a Queen
wearing their crown.

Inspirational Poems For Boys

Not with the get down, serious content with no frown.

But not all the time, your smile is like the rare season where the sun is barely shining, after the rain and clouds are gone.

A leader, a captain of your own time with depth, like the brass sound baritone in a live band.

The Magic of Believing

The Magic of Believing is having confidence in being different.

The path to independence is often with interference.

Watch where your footsteps lead you.

Goons & trouble makers watch to block the entrance.

Inspirational Poems For Boys

The Magic Of Believing will break through those dark seasons and dark people..

Cutting down & bagging up all the garbage.

We live among corrupt people at times who are living lavishly temporarily before they are locked up for treachery.

The Magic of Believing

They will be deceitful & selfish some ignorance from no faith and they WILL steal another's hard earned wealth.

Others who have sunk into the division among themselves may try to bring you down quietly.

Don't let outside forces stop the flow.
If it don't feel right it's not!!

The Magic of Believing

It's going to be tricky, so take your time to prepare as much as you can.

But guess what, You are so ready Freddy!!

The journey gets difficult, just stay on course. Weather those winter blizzards, so you can do cartwheels in the Sun or tippy toes on the moon while smiling! Believe in YOU!!

Keep Climbing

Bruised knees, dirty shoes, frustration sinking in negative attitudes.

Bruised hands, fatigued legs, searching & begging for a better way, an easier or quicker route, parched lips as you sip your water beverage, nearly out.

It looks so far away, how will we make it through the day.

Inspirational Poems For Boys

Grey clouds hid the sun, it's OK to rest, but your never done.

Just one, foot in front of the other young hearts, and just focus on today's travel.

The journey is the experience lived one day at a time.

So keep Climbing, with consistency you have already won!

Keep Climbing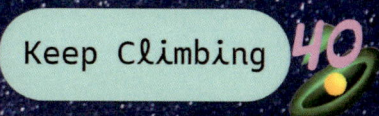

Post your flag on the mountain, and take in the view because you kept climbing.

Kept giving yoursel encouragement daily to strengthen your heart for the journey.

They will never tell you, but you are secretly motivating others around you. Thank you for Climbing this far. Keep Going!

Almost There

The pressure is hard here, you can feel it.

Just remember to breathe in those high tension challenging moments.

Almost There, but my arms are barely moving.

Space surfing energy is fading, so get anchored to positive thoughts as you sweat and labor for your passion.

Inspirational Poems For Boys

Your inner child says, don't complain & pace yourself in this race, it will help you reign over your Kingdom!

Don't sprint, jog with your earbuds in listening to your favorite song.

Kick off the run with everything within you. Focus & breathe before crossing the finish line to a victorious win.

Almost There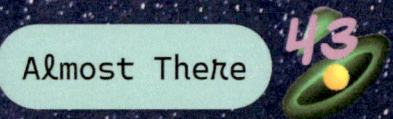

Congratulations you saw it through until the end. You're here and not with the quitters.
Break free of judgment, celebrate & sing out loud!

Almost There!!

No Limit's

You have potential like sugar that is unstirred at the bottom of the lemonade jug.

Your have great soil for growth. Please avoid bad seeds in the ground that listen to negative bugs.

Many will never understand their value and will move at the pace of a slug with No stars to chase.

Inspirational Poems For Boys

To manifest the Gold and treasures within, keep a shovel of faith to dig until ground breaks.

Until your purpose or mission is discovered, your future is safely locked away like,

Grandma's pumpkin-apple cookies and cake.

No Limits

Let your Faith manifest your sweetest destiny.

No limits, you can be whatever you set your heart & mind too.

No limits, even if it's been done again and again, they can't have your fingerprint Brand identity.

Be innovative & creative take advantage of programs.
No limits among the stars in outer space.

Inspirational Poems For Boys

47

Be an alien influencing others to change their Universe.

No limits among the stars in outer space.

Limit your time dwelling around negative spaces, people and things, that does not believe in your dreams, and know it's just a little fear creeping in.

Keep winners around you!
A team of masterminds looking for new planets of endless possibilities

No Limits in your Universe.

The Sky Is The Beginning

Clear blue skies, angelic songs the birds sings.

Peaceful clouds floating like birthday party balloons.

Filling you up with light, your vision is so amazing, funny & entertaining.

Moving in faith will help you maintain your focus.

Inspirational Poems For Boys

Stand still and feel the warmth from the gold sun.

It's like seeking the love from home cooked meals with a second and third plate.

Still emerging in experience & understanding, while your curiosity stirs your learning.

Keep flowing and growing with intentional force into your own Space.

The Sky is The Beginning

Then you'll see and pivot to new states of maturity, when

I tell you today that the, Sky is Only the Beginning!

So keep reaching, far like an Astronaut from Brooklyn soar to outer worlds.

Let's keep seeking and evolving into better versions of our old mental programing that's unfruitful & can not serve your new growth.

Inspirational Poems For Boys

The Sky is the beginning, let's space travel to different planets and galaxies to create better reality.

The Sky Is the beginning, there's a whole universe to create & explore.

Growing more and more as you reach for the stars so far, but are fantasies others wish were their realities.

Don't Forget To Plan

Humanity does not know your future!

One thing for certain is you will not `have one, unless you create a plan.

It's for the gift of our eyes and ears, to give ourselves over to learning to plan & map out our dreams!

Locate the Beginning at the start before your even start.

Inspirational Poems For Boys

So you can have a calculated decision that's smart.

Have a bird's eye view at the chess board, before a piece is played.

The same way the coach gets the team in practice everyday to plans for game day.

Don't Forget to plan, write down your vision & your goals.

Don't Forget To set long term & short term goals.

Dont Forget to Plan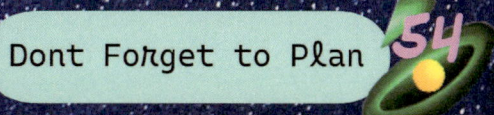

This will instill confidence & make you more bold.

Don't Forget to fold your clothes & keep your room neat & organized, your personal environment will set the tone.

A clutter house is a cluttered mind, unwritten thoughts is a confused closed mind.

Set the pencil to the pen, for clarity before you execute and begin.

      Don't Forget to Plan.

Don't Forget To Pray

Ambition like a pure white flame, within the fireplace of my heart it feels like home.

Seeking higher ground for clarity helps you tap into safe spaces to pray and strengthen your spirits.

Without God everything would be impossible, but with

Inspirational Poems For Boys

God all things are possible & ready to manifest.

Humbly avoid beating your chest, the presence relieves all stress, and in the Great I Am Majesty, I receive rest.

When confused & complexed, real guidance & strength will come from praying.

Hit your knees or fold your arms, sit still and hold tight and pray small prayer over your life.

Dont Forget to Pray

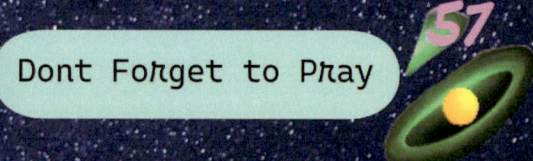

Don't Forget to Pray over your plans, so your Heavenly Father can rain down blessings & keep the favor and love flowing.

Don't Forget to Pray & Give gratitude for all the help.

For all gifts and talents, given to you at birth.

Don't Forget to Pray for your protection whenever you travel.

Inspirational Poems For Boys

Don't Forget to Praise him in troubled moments, know in these times it's working for your good in due time.

In all of your goals & endeavors and achievements, Don't Forget to Pray.

All life & blessings flows freely through him.

The Great I AM

Don't Forget To Study Hard

Even if you skip the line to the university, you can't escape the Universal Law of knowledge is necessary power for your journey

To give up the studious section of your gifts, will keep your energy low. Without insight to properly execute plans, you will lack tools & processing power.

Inspirational Poems For Boys

Hard head because you refuse to listen, unable to bust a move and quickly you start to lose.

Stay focus, all is not lost, you can change your course of direction.

Be patient, stay the course.
Work & study hard.
Keep tapping at the brick stony wall.

Don't Forget to Study Hard

A few more inches, before the treasure falls.

Pace your Breath. Let your progress gives you peace, to settle the anxiety and pressure.

Don't be surprised when others don't rejoice. Stay to yourself and prioritize your activities & goals.

Keep putting one foot in front of the other. Take it one day at a time.

Inspirational Poems For Boys

Failing to leverage time as a resource can cost and may add pressure.

Take a deep breath, make it a practice to retreat to a relaxed state of mind.

Set order like a gingerbread house, make sure you secure your heart again controversy winds and stand firm.

It's challenging, but just have a one bite at a time. Give yourself time to listen & digest.

Don't Forget to Study Hard

And pretty soon you'll start to earn, and become a positive influence to those who come around you.

When the seed becomes a tree, and the fruit is finally ripe, Success is like the sweet mango picked fresh from the tree.

Congratulations you stayed committed and saw it through until to the end!

The Beauty Of Your Imagination

Let's Fly to different galaxies.

Let's explore Life's shifting Realities

Let's go outside the neighborhood.

Let's go outside the norm.
Let's not remain dull.

Sharpen your wits and let your thoughts sway in the beautiful Tulip flowers.

Inspirational Poems For Boys

With all of those joyful ideas your mind will wander far from your creative pier, don't forget patience and protection.

Other wandering adventures in your imagination can be an alien jelly fish, a magical mermaids or a whimsical Ferris Wheels.

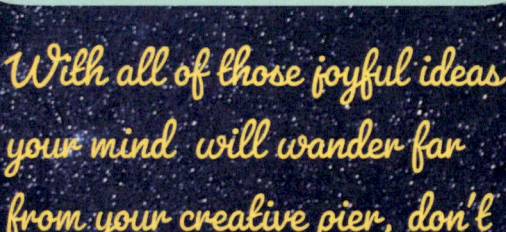

Encounter a new Universe and Pirate astronauts in spaceships. Exploring planets with living waters.

The Beauty Of Your Imagination 66

Keep a space in your heart for your imagination where creativity inhabits.

Practice visualizing positive images daily to visualize your future consistently.
Until you walk with the light breeze of your imagination, sitting under a beach umbrella with toes in the sand.

Until the sunrise and sunset becomes your daily routine and scenery.

Inspirational Poems For Boys

The heaviness of your eyelids start to snooze.

As the calm of the ocean wind blows through beach seashells into the creativity you hold.

Painting canvases from blank notebook thoughts, leaving it filled with color that emerges & intertwines.

The Beauty of Your Imagination, is the beauty of your mind.

The Beauty of Your Imagination

It's a rare jewels of pearls, locked in a shell resting on a ocean floor.

Unlock the mind & live limitless through the beauty of your imagination.

Soar High

Soar High towards the Ocean blue sky.
As free as the Eagles flies from the east, west & south side.

Soaring High above enemy lines, build castles to defend your life & the family name.

Soar High above the conflict, a bird's eye view perspective.

Don't wallow with the chickens. Don't get muddy with the piglets. Unless your starting a farm.

Inspirational Poems For Boys

Sour High above turbulence!

You were born to thrive above dark cloud comments & false roomers and yucky personalities.

Thunderstorms that leave you feeling gloomy in your bedroom.

Soar High

Just stand tall and stay strong.

Focus on YOUR mission. Massive action taken to hate BUT love the realities of success will always collide.

In the midst of persecution, a sign of transformation in the autumn season leaves will have you believing in better days.

For Soaring High

Peeling off old reptile Skin hibernating in greatness like a bear in its cave.

Inspirational Poems For Boys

The level of attack, will revive your value as an Eagle, overlooking the valley from the skyscraper mountain top in a tree planted in the stone.

Keep an appetite of royal excellence, you will never be prey because you will stay at the top of your world.

Gliding & swooping through the sky. Established Legacy as King of your own Galaxy

Soar High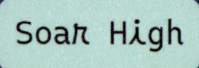

Focus on the love & the strength from your CORE it's a one of a kind source of GPS.

Admiration from the beauty of your wings when the sun shines upon you.

Ooh how the reflection of light glistens and dances among your thick coated feathers,

Leading the pack of Eagles that follows from the next generation.

Inspirational Poems For Boys

Victorious over the concrete jungle, letting your voice echo in the midst of the mumbo jumbo.

Freeing the misunderstood from the lies that are Loud forces, with their limiting beliefs always reach out for a healing reef.

Soaring High, to new levels and new depths.

Soar High

Soaring High among the clouds & trees.

Soaring High, you were born for this.
You waited & prepared your life for this.

Soar High like the Eagle effortlessly gliding through the wind, always continuing to thrive to be a champion.

Soar High.

Student

Don't get into a confined index of thinking.

To be a real scholar,

The World

is Your classroom.

From the bushel of autumn red, pink & yellow leafs.
To the pond where the toad lives.
To the lake, where the mountains watch the views.

Inspirational Poems For Boys

To the injustice & broke homes. Stolen jewels, by some cruel dudes..

Don't mingle with the wrong things, in the wrong places, at the wrong time you will find monsters with appetites that drools over your food!

Don't let them steal your plate.

Opponents really don't want duel, so they make issues then look around you and hide their hands.

Student

78

When you walk among the world, never consistently walk with your head down, keep your crown UP straight not down on devices. Kings walk with their head up.

Pay attention look around. Never go the same way twice.

You can do anything you set your mind to. Just change the questions of self doubts that you listen to.

Like, how can I get it done.

Student

Instead ask who has gotten it done, and find Mentors in your interest to follow and learn.

Whether a foreign language that speaks the language of love. Instrument that tells the vibe of our souls.

Or a teacher that has already traveled the road. Or fitness instructor for wellness health benefits

Be open to eating organic foods, drinking herbal teas, delicious

80

fruits in a smoothie to amuse your taste buds with delights of sunrise.

Our history isn't meant to create hate through emotionally lenses. Our history is to show our people stories of strength & resilience as a nation and the beauty of what togetherness hold.

Don't let the ugliness of other ruined the beauty inside you. Keep evolving, maturing, learning and becoming whole.
      Student

WATCH YOUR STEPS

JOURNAL
YOUR
JOURNEY
SEE
HOW FAR
YOU'VE COME

How Are We Doing

We hope you enjoyed our Inspirational Poems to inspire your journey!

Keep Dreaming Big & never give up on your gifts, talents & interest!

Scan the QR and leave comment or review at:

www.brooklynastronautent.com

HOPE YOU HAD A HAPPY DAY!

JOURNAL ABOUT GOOD DAYS TOO!